Newcastle between the Wars

Byron Dawson's Tyneside

Barras Bridge from the Hancock Museum, c.1938.

Newcastle between the Wars

Byron Dawson's Tyneside

Marshall Hall

Tyne Bridge Publishing

Acknowledgements

The author would like to thank the following for their help and encouragement in preparing this book for publication: Ray Marshall of the *Remember When* supplement to the *Evening Chronicle*, Newcastle; Marie-Thérèse Mayne, Laing Art Gallery, Tyne & Wear Archives & Museums, and the staff at Newcastle Libraries Local Studies. My thanks also to David Redpath, son of William Redpath, for permission to access his father's files regarding the artist, and Graham Dawson, a relative of the artist, for filling in previously existing gaps in his life from family records.

Unless otherwise indicated, colour illustrations ©Tyne & Wear Archives & Museums; photographs ©Newcastle Libraries. The line drawings appeared in the *North Mail and Evening Chronicle*. Our thanks to Tyne & Wear Archives & Museums and to ncjMedia. All efforts have been made to find original copyright holders of images reproduced.

Front cover: Watercolour of Fenwick's, Northumberland Street, Newcastle c.1938.
Frontispiece: The Haymarket c.1938.

Also by Marshall Hall: *The Artists of Northumbria*, 1973, 1982 and 2005; *The Artists of Cumbria*, 1979.

ISBN 978-1-857952-02-5

Published by
City of Newcastle upon Tyne,
Newcastle Libraries & Information Service,
Tyne Bridge Publishing, 2011

www.tynebridgepublishing.co.uk
www.newcastle.gov.uk/libraries

Printed by Elanders, North Tyneside

Market Street, Newcastle, 1935.

Discovering Byron Dawson

I love searching through the extensive archives of *Evening Chronicle* pictures, discovering long forgotten images, but I'm never so excited as when a new Byron Dawson drawing pops up. Photographs are a lovely window on the past, but a Byron Dawson drawing pulls you further in, gives you that 'I am there' feeling. He has a brilliant knack of weaving into his pictures what most artists struggle to find – atmosphere. There are many local areas I have rediscovered through the eyes and mind of Byron Dawson. He was the one who took me back to the days of the hustle and bustle of the Hoppings, the Quayside Market, St James's Park on a matchday and a boxing match at St James's Hall, where you could actually *taste* the atmosphere.

He could often be seen on the streets of Newcastle looking for his subject or subjects. If he was in a good mood you might receive a quick half smile as he trudged on, but however much you were willing to pay for a Byron Dawson drawing or painting, if he didn't like you there was no chance! They say he lived for beauty and certainly not for money. He would have little of it and never really wanted it – the picture of a true artist.

Ray Marshall, writer of the Evening Chronicle's 'Remember When' series.

The Cloth Market, from Mosley Street, August 24 1937.

Northumberland Street, c.1938

Based on his drawing 'An Impression of Christmas Shopping in Northumberland Street', published in December 1934, this scene, dominated by Fenwick's department store, is one to which Dawson returned several times. The original drawing, which appeared in the *North Mail*, led to several commissions, including one to paint the firm's original stores in Newcastle and Richmond in Yorkshire. J.J. Fenwick was originally from Richmond and opened a store on Northumberland Street in 1882 by combining two houses. These modest premises were rebuilt in 1913 to the design shown in this watercolour. By the mid-1930s, Northumberland Street was an increasingly busy section of the A1 Great North Road.

Byron Dawson, an artist on Tyneside

One morning in the mid-1920s a Newcastle newspaper editor and a young local artist went to the grounds of St Thomas's Church in Barras Bridge with the idea of a project to record the face of the city in a way that has never been done so comprehensively before, or since. The newspaper editor was William Redpath of the *North Mail and Newcastle Chronicle*, the artist was Byron Dawson and the project was to lead Dawson to draw just about every architectural landmark and street scene in his adopted city.

Born in Banbury, Oxfordshire in 1896, Dawson maintained throughout his professional life that he was an orphan. His mother had died in 1906, but in fact his father did not die until 1946. Dawson and his elder brother Horace were unofficially adopted by their mother's sister and her husband (a prison officer) and brought to Newcastle in 1910.

In 1925 Dawson was 29 and working as an assistant master of painting at Newcastle's Armstrong College (now Newcastle University) where he had studied fine art. William Redpath, an amateur artist himself, knew that Dawson desperately wanted a career as a professional artist and decided to help him by getting him to illustrate for the newspaper.

None of this would have been known had Redpath's son David not come across some notes among his father's papers when the grand old newspaperman died in 1985, at the age of 92. Redpath's efforts came just in time to raise Dawson's spirits, as he noted: 'The daughter of a famous Northumbrian family, a fine musician and a gifted sculptress, fell in love with him and his drawings. His friends believed that this would make him more disciplined and give him a real sense of responsibility, but it came to nothing. It was at this point I found the way to bring self-discipline and a regular income into his life.'

Redpath had fallen in love too, with Dawson's pencil drawings and watercolours of castles, cathedrals, ancient buildings and street scenes. 'If they could be translated into black and white – a difficult medium – I could see a way of using them.' Dawson appeared to like the idea – a godsend to any up-and-coming artist – but was doubtful whether he could do what was required. Redpath insisted he could, and to prove it 'We went together with our sketch books at five in the morning to Barras Bridge, Newcastle, did our drawings and went back to the studio to discuss the result. Mine was bolder, his more detailed – but I saw promise. There and then I commissioned a regular weekly feature for the Mail.'

However, 'this first drawing proved a greater problem for Dawson than he imagined. It was Monday. I wanted it delivered to me on Wednesday morning, in order to have a good line block made for Thursday's paper. Wednesday came. No Dawson. No drawing. I went to the studio and there was Dawson working furiously at his easel, with at least 20 large black and white drawings lying about the floor.

'"I can't do it," he woefully exclaimed. "It isn't like pencil drawing." I quickly glanced and picked out one.

'"You can't use that," he said, "it's no good."

'"It may not be the best," was my answer, "but this is what I want. Wait till you see it reduced and printed in the paper."'

This first of Dawson's drawings for the *North Mail* appeared on Friday October 9, 1925. Redpath could not have given him a better start as an illustrator. The study of the city's Bird and Fish Market was accompanied by a caption which described it as the work of 'Mr Byron Dawson, a rising Newcastle artist.' It was a great success.

The Newcastle scene that Dawson recorded over the next fourteen years was one still gripped by post-war gloom. The period between the two world wars was one of depression not only for the North East, but the nation as a whole. Newcastle, still very much a Victorian city, was particularly hard hit and it was not until a few years later that new construction projects such as the New Tyne Bridge, Carliol House, the Central Police Station, Market Street Fire Station, the new Newgate Street Co-operative Store and the New Medical School were initiated. All of these developments were recorded by Dawson along with studies of Newcastle's older buildings and street scenes.

Within weeks of his first *North Mail* success, Dawson became a familiar figure around the city, his drawing technique attracting as much interest as its subjects. The large size of his drawing board and the equally large piece of paper fixed to it intrigued everyone as, unusually for a street-scene artist, he always drew what can only be described as 'sight size' – putting onto paper the same size of image as he observed in real life.

The technique can be demonstrated by holding a finger parallel to a distant vertical object, noting its scale against the finger, and duplicating this scale on paper. Dawson was so skilled at this that he could – if challenged – take a small notepad, and drawing the façade of a building in fragments, starting left or right, top or bottom, put together the pieces of paper to form a complete and precisely interlocking image of the building!

Dawson produced hundreds of illustrations, and often with the ink barely dry on the hastily delivered sheets of half imperial paper, they made their appearance in the newspaper sometimes twice a week. Redpath continued to take a personal interest in them while he was editor of the newspaper, often suggesting the subject matter.

Byron's first study of the Bird and Fish Market on Clayton Street was very popular. The title of the first series – *Characteristic Corners of Newcastle* – produced all sorts of subjects such as Byker Bridge and the tower and entrance porch of St Andrew's Church – all with the flattering description in brackets below: 'Specially drawn for the *North Mail and Newcastle Chronicle* by Byron Dawson.'

Soon Dawson was able to give up his job at King's College and become a full-time professional artist – exactly as Redpath had hoped. The first thing he did was begin a painting commissioned by wealthy local art patron Major Robert Temperley. Temperley was so pleased with the result, a painting titled *Panel for*

Drawing Room, that he encouraged Dawson to show it at the Royal Academy exhibition of 1928. It was shown at the North East Coast Exhibition of the following year, and soon after Dawson was chosen to be one of several local artists to paint murals for the Laing Art Gallery.

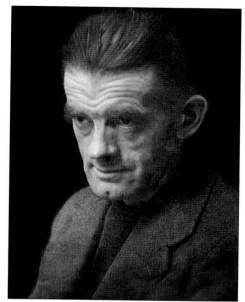

Byron Dawson (1896-1968).

Hard at work on his commission for the Laing – the largest painting of his whole career at more than 26 feet wide and titled: *John Baliol, King of Scotland, Doing Homage to King Edward I in the Great Hall of the Castle at Newcastle, in 1292* – he still found time to take up an offer from a local well-wisher to finance a painting trip to France, and was later able to spend some months painting in Gloucestershire. Even with the successful completion of his lunette for the Laing, the ready sale of his French and Gloucestershire watercolours, the acceptance by the Royal Academy in 1931 of his *Shepherd and Three Graces*, a major exhibition of his work at the Hatton Gallery, Newcastle in 1932, and his showing of three works at the Royal Scottish Academy in 1933, Redpath commissioned further illustrations for his newspaper to help Dawson financially.

Other series over the following years ranged from *An Artist Tours the Industrial North*, in which several Newcastle-based industries were featured, to *Newcastle's Changing Face*, illustrating new buildings in the city centre. Dawson's work for the *North Mail* ended in the autumn of 1939, eighteen months after William Redpath had fallen out with Lord Kemsley, the owner of the paper, and left the North East to become an editor in London. Short series had followed Redpath's departure, but when the *North Mail* amalgamated with *The Journal* in 1939, Dawson's services were discontinued.

During his years with the *North Mail* and *Sunday Sun*, Dawson drew just about everything there was to be drawn around Newcastle and produced occasional drawings of subjects as far afield as Teesside and Berwick. The *North Mail* was a regional newspaper and readers expected subjects from a wide area. By the time the series ended, he had not only a period of relative affluence to look back upon, but ready-made compositions for many of the watercolours both of Newcastle and the region he painted later.

Each of his drawings reproduced in the *North Mail* or *Sunday Sun* he carefully clipped out and gummed into old copies of *Braille News* donated by the Central Library Reading Room. So, if, as often happened shortly after a particular drawing had appeared in the paper, he was asked by a reader for a watercolour version, he could refer to his cuttings book for the composition. His watercolours of the Old Town Hall, Grainger Street, etc. reproduced in the following pages are all examples of this practise, and painted soon after the drawings had appeared, sometimes with slight changes to the detail.

As the 1930s drew to a close Dawson had reached the highpoint of his career as an illustrator. During the war years he relied mainly on his watercolours, and he was selected in the summer of 1940 to provide coloured illustrations for the *Recording Britain Scheme* funded by the Pilgrim Trust. These watercolours, which he painted in the Preston area, appeared in *Recording Britain*, published in 1947 by the Oxford University Press. He also continued to send work to the annual Artists of the Northern Counties exhibitions at the Laing Art Gallery.

After the war Dawson produced work for local glass company Reed Millican, spent some time as art master at Queen Elizabeth Grammar School, Hexham, and illustrated calendars for the Tyneside turbine-building giant Parsons'. Despite the income from these activities, a successful major exhibition of his work at the Shipley Art Gallery in 1955, and a commission in the same year to paint a large oil for the Laing's

Marshall Hall

The machine age: an illustration for a Parsons' calendar.

foyer depicting *Newcastle in the Reign of Elizabeth I*, his work quickly dwindled to an occasional view of two of his favourite subjects – Durham Cathedral and St Nicholas's Cathedral – a house study for a wealthy patron, a thematic oil for a pub, or a commission to draw some doomed building by the councils of Newcastle or Gateshead.

By the late 1950s it was clear that his best years as an artist were well behind him. Poor eating habits, excessive smoking and irregular sleep had taken their toll so much that he was occasionally mistaken for a tramp.

Loyal friends patiently trudged up the long flight of stairs to his studio to offer him work or to buy what he might have just painted, but to no avail. Indeed, by the time I joined him as a pupil in the late 1950s he was already a shadow of the virile, auburn-haired man he had been.

Dawson in his studio in Saville Row in the 1950s.

We first met when he had just turned sixty, and became not only master and pupil, but firm friends. He overheard me one day in his usual lunchtime haunt – the New Bridge Street Cafeteria – proudly discussing an illustration I had been commissioned to do for a local magazine, some months previously, and how I wished I had been able to get additional work from its publishers.

He modestly introduced himself as someone who had done a 'bit of illustration' himself, and suggested I bring a copy of the magazine along to his Saville Row studio so that he could see what I had done. His reaction to my tiny drawing was to look at it intently for a minute then reach into a pile of books and papers next to his drawing board, extract an old copy of *Braille News* and hand it to me without comment.

'What do you think?' he asked, as I turned its pages and found myself looking at cuttings of drawing after drawing. I glanced up at him and found a look of eager anticipation on his face.

'They're fantastic, but I'll never be able to draw like this.'

'We shall see,' he replied, though I'll have to make a small charge for showing you how.'

In the event I became as much his assistant as pupil, mounting his sheets of watercolour paper onto his drawing board, cleaning his brushes, and running errands for his materials.

By the time I ended my association with him I had become suspicious that he was sleeping in his studio. A makeshift bed in the corner, the remains of a hurried breakfast when I arrived for a morning lesson, and an awareness that his tiny electric fire had been on much longer than might have been expected at that early hour bore testimony to this conclusion.

'It's not so bad,' he said cheerfully when he realised I had discovered his secret. 'And besides, it means I don't have to travel very far to work!'

Eventually a friend arranged for him to live and work in Newcastle's historic Plummer Tower, recently annexed by the Laing as a museum, and it was here that Redpath found him when he visited Newcastle in 1965.

Dawson wrote to him afterwards: 'It was a very pleasant surprise when you walked into Plummer Tower. Seeing you again after so many years took me back to those days when life was so full of meaning and the years ahead appeared so promising. Since then I have lost some of my enthusiasm altho' it is not to be wondered at.'

In the following year, and after months of poor health Dawson was admitted to Wooley Sanatorium in the Tyne Valley for a major chest operation. He was never to leave it and died two years later, probably from TB, at the age of almost 72.

There were several obituaries in the local press, and one in particular – *The Journal*, 15 February 1968 – contained one of the

William Redpath during his visit to Newcastle, 1965.

most accurate pen portraits of the artist in later life. Written by a friend of many years, and well-known reporter for the paper, Richard Martin, it described him as 'the shy artist'.

'He shunned the public and publicity with horror. Yet he was one of the most brilliant artists the North has produced. His work was so distinctive that he did not need to sign it. His style was such that his signature was not needed to identify it.

'He looked the part, too. His hair was usually unkempt, he never wore a hat and he walked the city streets in a long overcoat which had seen better days, so that few city dwellers recognised him for who he was. His eyes, however, were a part of him that were still remarkably alive, even in the last stages of the illness which claimed him.

'Under his sometimes unprepossessing exterior he was a delightful man, lovably stubborn, he would not work for anyone whom he did not like and very often this was to his considerable loss, for his style of living was never – by his own choice – other than spartan.'

During his lifetime Dawson saw his beloved Newcastle change enormously, but while he died in near poverty, and now lies in an unmarked grave in St Andrew's Cemetery in Jesmond, he has left us a priceless legacy of images of the city as it looked between the two world wars that shaped the history of our nation in the twentieth century.

Marshall Hall, 2011

Pilgrim Street, 1935

One of the most dramatically transformed, and crowded, streetscapes in Newcastle in the late 1920s and early 1930s was the section of Pilgrim Street between New Bridge Street and Worswick Street. This watercolour was based on Dawson's drawing of 1935 under the banner SOME OF NEWCASTLE'S LATEST BUILDINGS. It shows Carliol House, 1928 (centre), and the new Police Headquarters, Magistrates' Court and Fire Station, 1931-33 (right). Beyond Carliol House is the Paramount Cinema (later the Odeon). Not only were these buildings the most modern in the city, but the most prominently visible. Thanks to the New Tyne Bridge which opened in 1928, this part of Pilgrim Street had become 'The Gateway to Newcastle'. Thousands queued for the Paramount, often right down the street, and hundreds of people called at the ground floor showrooms of the Newcastle upon Tyne Electric Supply Company, who owned Carliol House, to see the latest gadgets.

The Royal Arcade, Pilgrim Street, late 1920s

When the Royal Arcade, the John Dobson-designed building on the left, opened in 1832, Pilgrim Street was still enjoying its reputation as the city's finest thoroughfare. When Dawson drew the sketch upon which this watercolour is based, in 1926, the street had long fallen from grace, having been outclassed by Grey Street. The Royal Arcade was intended to be Newcastle's first interior market or exchange, but it never fulfilled its expectations. It was too far from the best shopping streets and too near to rundown housing at the edge of the town centre. It became increasingly neglected until it was demolished in the 1960s to make way for the Central Motorway (East). It was intended to reconstruct the Arcade elsewhere in the city and each stone was carefully chalk-marked to enable this, but the scheme never came to anything. Instead a 'sorry imitation' was designed into Swan House and some of the stones of the Arcade ended up in Heaton Park.

St James's Park, late 1930s

One of the most popular and avidly scrutinised of any of Dawson's drawings for the *Sunday Sun* in the late 1930s, this watercolour interpretation didn't reveal the original's secret until more than thirty years later when it went on display at the Laing Art Gallery. A sharp-eyed visitor noticed that there are twelve Newcastle players on the pitch instead of the usual eleven! In fact Newcastle United could have done with an extra player in those days. Relegated for the first time in the 1933-34 season, its performance had been far from impressive. In the 1937-38 season the team, according to a club history, was 'saved from the drop by a whisker'.

In the following season the Football League was suspended when war broke out and not properly reinstated for the next seven years. Friendly games were played, but did not attract the crowds evident in this illustration.

This hallowed piece of Newcastle originated in 1882 as a pitch surrounded by earth banks. By the 1930s it had been developed into the 60,000 (standing) capacity stadium in the watercolour. Proposals to increase this capacity by another 20,000 were put forward in 1950, but it was not until 1973 that a new stand was added to the Leazes side. Today the stadium that dominates Newcastle's skyline boasts a seating capacity of almost 53,000.

Bigg Market, c.1936

The news vendor in the foreground, and the handful of stalls beyond, give clues to the day and time at which this watercolour of the Bigg Market was painted: late Saturday afternoon when the number of stalls had dwindled, and the *Chronicle Late Night Extra* was on sale to homeward-bound shoppers. Painted some ten years after the drawing on page 50, Bainbridge's department store entrance is to the left, a popular shortcut to Market Street. The first floor restaurant offered an unrivalled view of the Market from tables served by immaculately turned-out waitresses.

It is a scene which Jack Common in *Kiddar's Luck* might have been describing: 'My last call was again at the Bigg Market to see what I would pick up. The stalls were being dismantled now; a fancy box, some bruised fruit or something of real value that had been overlooked among the straw, paper and boxes.'

Grainger Street West, c.1935

The section of Grainger Street West in this watercolour was very familiar to Dawson, although its main attractions are just out of view beyond the corner of what was then the Gas Board showroom visible in the near distance. At 7, 9 and 11 were the galleries of Mawson Swan & Morgan which sold his work throughout his career, while next door was the artists' materials supplier, the North of England School Furnishing Company. The gallery would often give the artist an advance on the sale of his work while the shop, in his later years, allowed him generous time to settle bills.

The Mawson Swan & Morgan branch did not survive very long after Dawson's death in 1968. Its manager (and friend of the artist) moved to Collingwood Street, where he opened the Morgan & Brown gallery. The North of England School Furnishing Company also closed along with the Gas Board showroom and its offices. On the other side of the street, Harker's – once one of the city's leading office and home contract furnishers, whose delivery van is on the left – vacated its huge premises on the street in the 1970s. The wall of St John's Church, in the foreground, has now been replaced by a paved square.

St Nicholas's Cathedral and Square c.1939

One of more than 200 images of St Nicholas's Cathedral which Dawson either drew or painted during his career as an artist, this view from the east was his favourite. The inclusion of the office buildings to the west, and along Collingwood Street, meant that businessmen with premises there liked to have examples hanging behind their desks, so there was a ready sale. When he first painted this scene the Square looked much as it had done for decades. The Old Town Hall still stood on the extreme right, and a modern office block on the corner of St Nicholas Street and Collingwood Street had yet to replace the old buildings beyond the trolley bus in the watercolour.

In the 1950s the area immediately in front of the Cathedral was transformed by the raising of the area around Queen Victoria's statue (centre) to prevent parking, and the whole area is today being redeveloped as part of a programme to reinvigorate the Cathedral and surroundings.

The Town Hall, mid-1930s

Given the impressive appearance of the building in this watercolour and its trifling cost by today's standards of £50,000, Newcastle's 'new' Town Hall caused plenty of controversy even before its completion in 1863. John Dobson said: 'The hideous town hall would ruin the character of what might have been one of the finest streets in the kingdom.' Queen Victoria's statue in the foreground, unveiled in 1903, proved only a little less controversial when the popular Rutherford Memorial Fountain which had occupied the site since 1894 was relocated to the Bigg Market.

The Town Hall was replaced by a modern office block in the 1970s (after the new Civic Centre had opened on Barras Bridge) so the scene today is very much less impressive than in Dawson's time. The office block has seen various occupants since its completion – even acting as a substitute main post office when the nearby St Nicholas's Post Office closed.

Swinburne Place c.1934

One of the lesser known backwaters of the city, Swinburne Place, behind Westgate Road, provided the type of subject that Dawson delighted in. This view looking west to St Matthew's Church, and Summerhill Street, is within yards of one of Newcastle's busiest thoroughfares. Reached via a narrow cobbled lane, the line of 1820s buildings on the right looks down on a scene which even today surprises visitors with its tranquillity.

Beyond the railings on the left is a pleasant open public area – a legacy of the last will and testament of one Hadwin Bragg, owner of nearby Summerhill House, who was determined it remain much as it looked when he gazed upon it from his own windows. On the further side of the area lies Summerhill Grove, one-time home of the Richardson family of leather manufacturers of whom a great-grandson was the late actor Sir Ralph Richardson. The houses pictured are still occupied by families, although Ravensworth Terrace, which continues up to the church, once incorporated a synagogue later used as a photographic studio.

Lovaine Place c.1939

Built in the early 1820s, at the same time as the distantly visible St Thomas's Church was being constructed, this early morning scene with its milk delivery cart in the foreground was one very familiar to Dawson. He lived here for a brief period in one of the substantial, three-storey buildings with the wrought iron balconies, by which time most had been deserted by the type of family for which they were originally built. Lovaine Place, later joined by Lovaine Terrace and Lovaine Crescent, were built to accommodate Newcastle's expanding middle-class population and anticipated the building of further such housing in nearby Jesmond.

All of these streets were demolished to make way for the building of the city's Civic Centre, opened in 1968, and Newcastle's Polytechnic, 1969, leaving only this watercolour and the several others of the area he painted in subsequent years, to remind us of its one-time peaceful existence only a few hundred yards from the bustle of the Haymarket.

The Empire Theatre, Newgate Street, late 1930s

The closure of Newcastle's Empire Theatre on Newgate Street in 1963 effectively meant the end of variety shows in the city. Originally an old coach house dating from the mid-nineteenth century, the Empire of this watercolour, had, since its doors opened in 1903, become one of the north's major venues for the nation's top stars. Joe Loss, Arthur Askey, Tommy Trinder and Max Miller were just some of the names on a star-studded list of performers. Two years after the theatre's closure this part of the street was redeveloped to accommodate the Newgate Shopping Centre and the Swallow Hotel. On the opposite side of the street, where part of the former Rutland furniture shop is visible, there is now a bakery. The Rose and Crown pub, once the next-door neighbour of the Empire, still stands today.

Northumberland County HQ and Moot Hall, 1934

In 1934 this building, the Northumberland County Headquarters, recently extended upwards from the original 1910 structure, was opened by President of the Board of Trade, Sir Walter Runciman. The scene has changed little today. The Northumberland HQ became redundant following the creation of the new county of Tyne & Wear in 1974 and later relocated to Morpeth. Between 1988 and 1993 the building was converted into the Vermont Hotel, of which six storeys face the historic Moot Hall, and the remaining four descend to the Side. The Moot Hall (to the left of the hotel), was completed in 1812 as the Northumberland County Court & Prisons. It was designated a Crown Court in 1980.

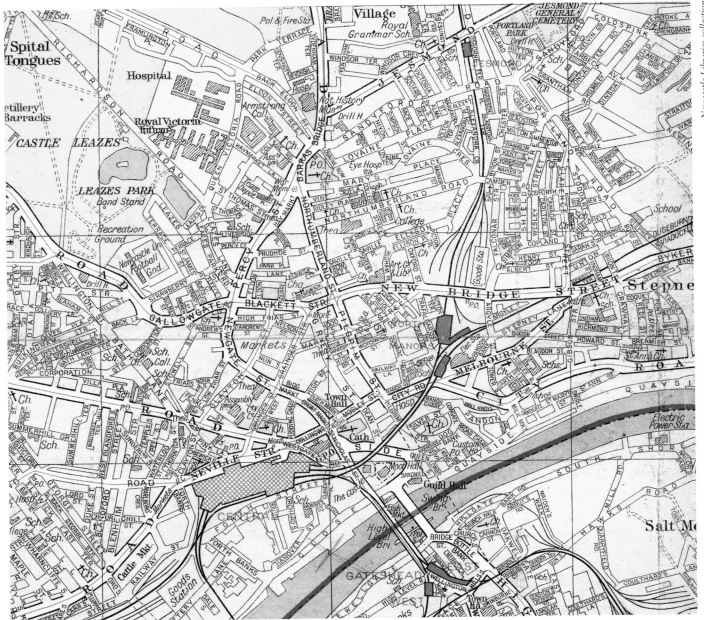

This map, reproduced from a Geographia publication dated 1927, shows us Byron Dawson's Newcastle. The New Tyne Bridge, which would open in 1928, is marked as a dotted line. Many of the streets marked on the map, from Silver Street to Lovaine Place, have now vanished beneath the redevelopment of the city, but were recorded by Dawson before they disappeared forever.

The Bird and Fish Market, St Andrew's Street – Clayton Street, 1925

This 'striking sketch' was the first of Dawson's illustrations for the *North Mail*, appearing on 9 October, 1925. As novelist Jack Common would recall of his boyhood visits to the Bird Market, in *Kiddar's Luck*: 'An incredible joint that. It stood on the corner above the Fish Market … A narrow staircase led up to this place, and so many people were coming and going upon it, you would find yourself halted on one foot before the other could get a toe-hold between several sets of heels.' Unlike the Fish Market below, of course, the species on display were not dead and waiting to be consumed, but very much alive. 'The walls were hung with tiers of cages, most of them tiny, which contained a variety of flutter connected with canaries, linnets, and finches, bull, gold or green all singing madly so as to get themselves sold quick.'

By the mid-1970s the two markets had completely disappeared to make way for the Eldon Square shopping development. The only surviving building in the drawing is the former Lord Collingwood pub, whose bow front can be seen centre. Known at the time of the drawing, and for many years subsequently as the Fish Bar because of its proximity to its neighbour, it went on to house an amusement arcade.

Central Station Portico, 1926

When Dawson drew this view of the portico of Newcastle's Central Station, he could not have imagined that one of his major oil paintings would one day grace the walls of its magnificently tiled refreshment room (his view of the North Tyne in what is now the Centurion Bar).

The railway station would become all too familiar to him over the following years as he used it regularly to travel to Durham City to draw and paint its Cathedral and Castle, eventually producing more studies of these buildings than possibly any other artist in history.

The paper's caption to his drawing of the portico said that 'one of the main features which strikes the visitor to Newcastle is the handsome portico of the Central Station,' and it was 'something of which every Novocastrian can be proud.' This still holds true today, notwithstanding that the foreground of the drawing is now occupied by rail users' parked cars, and bus shelters, and the further end of the portico lined by waiting taxis

Percy Street, 1936

A favourite subject of famous Newcastle artist Ralph Hedley (1848-1913), the antique shop in the foreground of this drawing survived as part of a group of early eighteenth-century buildings until the 1960s. The shop, whose furniture for sale was invariably on display on the cobbles in front of the building, had been owned by the city's Macdonald family for several years. A greengrocer and fresh fish shops were nearby. Dawson occasionally visited the shop to share a pot of tea with Macdonald senior, and later his son Norman, and would sometimes buy old oil paintings to overpaint with his own compositions. He found this cheaper than buying new, unused canvases!

The shops were replaced in the 1960s by the main city branch of Barclays Bank. Norman carried on the family business in a shop below the railway viaduct at the top of The Side. He called it Dog Leap Antiques because of its proximity to Dog Leap Stairs, and one of his specialities was prints of old Newcastle, among these Dawson's etched versions of his *North Mail* drawings.

The red brick bulk of Eldon Square now towers over the right-hand side of the street, opposite where the old antique shop once stood, with Eldon Garden further along Percy Street.

Brunswick Place, 1937

When Brunswick Chapel was built, this short lane at the south end of Northumberland Street not only became home to the principal Methodist church in the district, but also to the Northumberland Institution for the Promotion of the Fine Arts in the North of England. When the drawing was published in 1937 the Chapel was still vigorously fulfilling its original function, but No. 3 Brunswick Place, in which the founder of the Institution, artist Thomas Miles Richardson (1784-1848), staged his exhibitions from 1822-1827, had long been demolished. A plaque on the right-hand side of the street, where Fenwick's is today, later marked its one-time occupation by the artist, but that has also now vanished. Next to Brunswick Chapel, on the right, is the Brunswick Chapel Lecture Hall.

Opposite Fenwick's was the Bernard J. Stone Art Gallery. This gallery, which later moved to Ridley Place, and after that to St Mary's Place, would help establish the reputation of several now famous local artists, including Norman Cornish.

Northumberland Street in 1938 with southbound Gateshead and Newcastle trams, pursued by a Newcastle trolleybus on route 9 (Osborne Road – Central Station). The shop at the corner of Blackett Street and Northumberland Street is the department store Lowe and Moorhouse. Beyond is Woolworth's and Brunswick Place. No wonder the illustration of Brunswick Place, opposite, was printed under the headline WHERE TRAFFIC'S ROAR IS NEAR!

Bessie Surtees House, Sandhill, 1934

This Quayside scene might date from the nineteenth rather than the twentieth century. Cattle and sheep were still being driven through the city as late as 1934. But it was the buildings that captured Dawson's imagination. Bessie Surtees House, and the buildings immediately beside it were quaint enough to fascinate any artist. These homes of rich local merchants, built in the Tudor period, later became shops, business premises and cafés. Now a Grade I listed building, Bessie Surtees House (at the far left of the drawing) is the North East Regional Office of English Heritage. It is famous for the elopement of Bessie Surtees with John Scott on 18 November, 1772.

The cattle were heading towards a market on the western fringe of the city, off Scotswood Road. It survived until after the Second World War, having served the local farming community and the Tyneside butchery trade for more than a century.

St Mary's Place, 1936

When this drawing was published under the headline NEW TOWN HALL MIGHT BE BUILT HERE
nobody could have predicted that some thirty years would go by before it would actually be completed.
Although an open competition for what later became known as the Civic Centre was launched in 1939, the
outbreak of the second world war caused the project to be abandoned.

Lovaine Hall, the imposing building on the right of the drawing was still a venue for many social
occasions in the mid-1930s and the quiet street housed a number of artists' studios. It was not until 1958
that the scene began to change noticeably and continued until the completion of the Civic Centre in 1968.

Today the street is busier than at any time in its previous history, with hundreds of students from the
nearby University of Northumbria and heavy traffic. John Dobson Street, a latter-day addition to the city's
road network now intersects St Mary's Place just some 50 metres west of the point where Dawson's drawing
was made around three-quarters of a century ago on the corner of College Street.

St Mary's Roman Catholic Cathedral, Clayton Street West, 1937

By the time this drawing was published in 1937, as part of his *Religion and Commerce* series, Dawson was involved in a long flirtation with Catholicism that lasted until his death. One of his greatest friends and supporters in later life was Father Harriot of St Andrew's Roman Catholic Church in Worswick Street, who conducted the artist's funeral service.

St Mary's was completed in 1842 (though the tower and steeple were not added until 1872) and has been a cathedral since 1850. Today, the boundary wall to the cathedral, in the foreground, has been remodelled to make steps up to a bronze statue of Cardinal Basil Hume.

Bewick Street on the right was named after the North East's first great illustrator Thomas Bewick, who lived nearby. A bronze relief of Bewick's famous Chillingham Bull has now been set into the pavement on the right of the drawing.

The Theatre Royal, 1935

Many earlier views of the Theatre Royal had been taken from Grey Street looking up towards the building instead of from the corner of Grey Street and Market Street, so this illustration was celebrated as from 'a new viewpoint'. In 1935 the theatre was the city's premier venue for plays, operatic and ballet performances, as it is today. It was built because Richard Grainger demolished the first Theatre Royal on Mosley Street as he redeveloped the whole area. Grainger compensated the owners generously and the new theatre opened in 1837.

The drawing shows a theatre which, despite public opposition to it being built at all, is regarded as 'the greatest building on Grey Street' and is now a Grade I listed building. It has undergone a number of facelifts. In 1986-88 the 1,200-seater interior was restored and remodelled, extensions to its original floor plan were carried out along Market and Shakespeare Streets, and the staircase was improved. Further refurbishment took place in 2000 into Market Street and the Royal, one of the largest traditional theatres in Britain, is undergoing a £4.75m revamp during 2011, ensuring that it will continue as a major attraction.

Byker Bridge, 1926

Few parts of Newcastle have changed so dramatically in character as the area below Byker Bridge. Erected in 1878 to save pedestrians and traffic having to descend the steep sides of the lower Ouseburn before climbing to either Newcastle town centre or Byker, the bridge spanned an area of factories and slums crowding the banks of what was virtually an open sewer. Jack Common, writing of the scene from the bridge in his semi-autobiographical sequel to *Kiddar's Luck*, *The Ampersand*, wrote: 'The Ouseburn wound like the sloughed-off skin of a yellow snake among abattoirs and factories and cobbled streets, past brick ruins and village rows.'

Who could have forseen that this same area would one day be transformed into one of the city's most exciting cultural destinations? The whole area has been transformed by the progressive cleaning of the stream, (a pair of otters has been sighted in it recently), the planting of trees and the creation of grassed areas, until today it is virtually unrecognisable.

The Black Gate, Castle Garth, 1935

This tiny oasis of peace, in one of the busiest areas of Newcastle, proved a magnet to the unemployed and homeless of the 1930s as a daytime and occasional night-time refuge. The old building, built between 1247 and 1250, but much altered over the years, was still recovering from years of chequered occupation which had seen it serving as a tenement and even a pub, The Two Bulls Heads. In the early 1880s the tenants had moved out of what had become a virtual slum, and after restoration it became the Museum of the Newcastle Society of Antiquaries. Over the years the Society's magnificent collection of antiquarian objects and books grew, until in 2009 most of the exhibits were moved to the Great North Museum Hancock.

The Black Gate takes its name not from the blackening of the exterior by years of pollution, but because it was bought by a wealthy merchant, Patrick Black, during the Civil War. The foreground area has now been re-landscaped and grassed over.

The Hancock Museum, Great North Road, 1935

This monument to the memory of naturalist brothers John and Albany Hancock, which opened in 1878, has now been transformed into the Great North Museum Hancock.

Drawn from a corner of Jesmond Road, the illustration captures a scene that changed dramatically in the early 1970s as this area was remodelled for the Central Motorway (East). The Museum's entrance was repositioned to Claremont Road, the bronze eagles by John Hancock that adorned its gateposts were split between the Hancock and the Discovery Museum, and its handsome lamps moved to the front of the building – only to be stolen soon afterwards!

The building featured in several of Dawson's later drawings for the *North Mail*, and on one occasion he used it as a vantage point from which to draw the Haymarket (see frontispiece). Fascinatingly, the caption to one of his drawings of the building and its grounds, featured in the newspaper four years later, asked what could be done to improve both the Hancock and the Haymarket. He probably would have approved of Great North Museum Hancock.

Grey's Monument, 1937

Erected in 1838, Grey's Monument had long been the city's most famous landmark. Dawson had already included it in several of his previous drawings for the *North Mail* but on this occasion decided to give it the full prominence it deserved. Beyond the monument, the busy building scene shows the construction of Grainger House, destined to accommodate the Grainger Trust, Lamb & Edge the estate agents, and a new post office for the city describing itself as a Post, Money, Order & Telegraph Office.

Little was to change until the 1970s, when the YMCA building towering to the left of the Monument was taken down to make way for the Eldon Square shopping development and replaced with a shiny glass entrance. In 1981 Monument Metro Station arrived below and to the right of the Monument, and the Monument Mall shopping development would later replace Grainger House. On the far right of the view is Mawson Swan & Morgan's gift shop of the day.

Ellison Place, 1936

Ellison Place has changed so much since this illustration was produced that it is almost unrecognisable today. It was home to the city's Mansion House (in the middle distance), until the 1950s. By the 1930s the houses were principally business quarters, but a few well-off people still lived there, including so many medical men that it was known as 'Doctors' Row'.

All this changed with the building of an access road between John Dobson Street and the Central Motorway (East), which scythed through the area. Where Dawson stood to make his drawing is now MEA House, completed in 1974. Beyond it, immediately to the south-east, the Church of the Divine Unity, built in the late 1930s still survives, but the terrace is now part of Northumbria University.

A reminder of the street's one-time identity as 'the gentlest and best-built part of the town' is a blue plaque on the wall of No 4, marking the birthplace on 2 March 1923 of Cardinal Basil Hume, son of eminent physician William Errington Hume. The plaque was placed on the building following the Cardinal's death in 1999. Cardinal Hume was created Archbishop of Westminster and then a Cardinal in 1976.

St James's Hall, Strawberry Place, 1936

When this drawing was published as part of the *Sunday Sun*'s '*How the North Lives and Plays*' series St James's Hall was still enjoying its status as the main venue for boxing matches in the North East. It opened on 12 May 1930 as the 'New' St James's Hall to distinguish it from the 1909 building it replaced in Gallowgate, next to St James's football ground. Its well-planned seating allowed every spectator to have a good view, so it was quickly established as one of the most popular sporting venues on Tyneside. Originally built as a dedicated boxing stadium, within a year it was also promoting a new sport – all-in wrestling.

As the decade progressed, boxing matches began to feature less frequently but all-in wrestling became a regular Saturday night event until the hall closed as a sporting venue in 1968. By then the building had deteriorated considerably and was barely able to pay its way. The last boxing event took place on 22 May 1967, and the last wrestling bout followed on 27 January 1968. Top of the bill was the infamous Jackie Pallo, who predictably won by two falls. The owners, the Essoldo Group cinema chain, made it a bingo hall, and so it remained until the end of its days. The building was demolished in 1976 to make way for St James's Metro Station.

Nelson Street, 1937

The fruit and veg vendors in this scene may have since moved to slightly different locations, but this junction between Nelson Street and Clayton Street remains just as busy as when the drawing was published. Standing today where he drew his sketch, with his back to the Lord Collingwood pub, Dawson would see that the space between the rounded end building on the left, and what were once the walls of High Friar Street, has now been filled by the Eldon Square shopping development. The north side of Nelson Street today conceals architectural alterations to what is simply a façade. The one-time Gaiety Cinema's projecting canopy in the middle distance has long departed. The nearby Café Royal pub was one of Dawson's favourites in the late 1920s and early 1930s, when it was popular with intellectuals and fellow artists.

In the distance can be seen the upper end of Grainger Street and Central Exchange Buildings, which once housed one of Newcastle's earliest art exhibition venues, the Central Exchange News Room and Art Gallery. A catastrophic fire gutted the interior in 1901. The central space reopened in 1906 as the Central Arcade, one of whose arched entrances just peeps into the distance.

Higham Place, 1936

Higham Place was once a busy thoroughfare connecting Ellison Place to New Bridge Street and containing the main entrance to the Laing Art Gallery. The doorway second down on the left was the entrance to Newcastle's Pen & Palette Club, founded in 1900. In the distance is architect John Dobson's Lying-in Hospital, opened in 1826, and moved to Jubilee Road in 1923. By 1936 it had been the home of the BBC's North East studios for eleven years. In 1988 the studios moved to Spital Tongues. Today the last buildings on the left have been replaced by Higham House and the Laing's public entrance has been moved round the corner to New Bridge Street. The Lying in Hospital is now surrounded by Portland House.

Dawson had close connections with both the Laing and the Pen & Palette Club. The Laing's curator Bernard Stevenson paved the way to several purchases for the gallery, most notably his lunette *John Baliol, King of Scotland ...* , and Dawson was an honoured guest at the club on many occasions. A final connection was the Northern Architectural Association at No. 6.

Silver Street, 1926

Once the residence of Henry Bourne, one of Newcastle's earliest and greatest historians, Silver Street had long been a slum area by the time this illustration appeared in the winter of 1926. Dawson was attracted to it because this area at the foot of Pilgrim Street was disappearing as a result of the clearance of buildings to make way for the New Tyne Bridge. His view of the corner of the street where it dipped towards Pandon Dene and Newcastle Quayside suggests that time had already anticipated the breaker's hammer, the gap between the lamp-post on the left and the shop-fronted block in the middle distance showing only the remains of one of the ancient buildings which once stood there.

Not much of this street, named after the Jewish silver dealers who traded there, survived except All Saints' Church, whose steeple dominates the location. The church was deconsecrated in 1961, then reopened in 1996 as St Willibrord with All Saints Anglican Catholic Church.

Dean Street, 1937

In 1937 the Quayside was still the commercial heart of the city, Dean Street itself forming part of this heart, with Cathedral Buildings (1901) on the right, and Milburn House (1902-5), lower down, full to capacity with the offices of ship and colliery owners, timber and coal merchants, solicitors and accountants – most associated in some capacity with the busy Port of Newcastle only a few hundred yards away through the soaring railway viaduct at the foot of the street.

The Milburn family, rich through shipping and coal, financed the construction of Milburn House. Its floors are identified like the decks of an ocean liner, with 'A' for the top floor and 'G' for the bottom floor. One of the eighteenth-century buildings on the left – No. 42, just beside the first parked car in the drawing – would have interested Dawson if he'd lived longer. In 1971 it became the Dean Gallery, which would not only sell his work but in 1993, in collaboration with the author, staged the artist's first major retrospective exhibition, with over fifty of his works on show. Beyond the gallery (which closed in 2003) a major change to the street of earlier date was the demolition of several buildings on the left to give access to a multi-storey car park, later infilled over the entrance with a mock Georgian façade.

Plummer Tower, Croft Street, 1938

Little could Dawson have imagined, when he drew the city's medieval Plummer Tower, that he would one day live in the eighteenth-century brick-built addition to the ancient building. It was then occupied by the National Union of Seamen, but in 1962 the nearby Laing Art Gallery took possession of it as an annexe. The building required a caretaker and Dawson was invited to fulfil the role in return for free lodgings. The impetus for this generous offer came from the Laing's curator Collingwood Stevenson, who had taken a kindly interest in the artist for many years. Dawson spent three of what he would describe as the happiest years of his life in the building until his last illness. Later, Dawson's friend and gifted amateur artist Joseph Kirsop would come to live in the cramped but adequate accommodation. The building survives as one of only two, two-storey former towers along the one-time town walls, the other being Sallyport Tower.

St Matthew's Church, Summerhill, 1937

Part of a group of buildings that greeted the eye of visitors from the west of the city, St Matthew's Church and the headquarters of the North East Savings Bank, made an attractive subject and like several earlier Dawson illustrations in the *North Mail*, readers could purchase it as a print for 2s 6d in aid of the *Chronicle* Sunshine Fund.

The CHURCH THAT TOWERS OVER NEWCASTLE was completed in 1895 at the top of Summerhill Street, providing an important landmark and popular place of worship for locals. The density of the local population in 1937 is evident in the activity in the foreground, with a post office and shops, as well as the Savings Bank to the left, doing brisk business. This junction of Westgate Road, and Elswick Road was very busy even in the 1930s so the Council provided a towering source of illumination that gave the area a name that survives among older city residents today – The Big Lamp. The traffic has increased enormously, but the busy pedestrian scene of the drawing has all but disappeared. St Matthew's is now the Church of St Matthew with St Philip and St Augustine.

Newgate Street Co-op Store, 1926

Just around the corner from his studio at 122 Newgate Street in the mid-1920s, this view gives a rare glimpse of Newcastle's original 1870s Co-op Store. This scene was one of the busiest in the city, the junction between St Andrew's Street in the foreground and Newgate Street at right angles, a melée of handcarts and horse carts shuttling between the former Wholesale Fruit & Vegetable Market and what was then a major cross-town thoroughfare.

St Andrew's Street was swallowed up in 1971 by the Eldon Square shopping development and its more recent additions. The magnificent Co-op's future is also now in question since the closure of all but its food hall in 2009. Rebuilt in 1931-2 to its familiar design of today it is one of the city's finest interwar buildings.

An interesting feature of the scene is Newcastle's first wireless shop, opened to take advantage of the growing popularity of broadcasting, on the right. It was relocated to Gallowgate when its site, along with those of neighbouring shops, was needed for the rebuilding of the Co-op.

The Lit and Phil, late 1920s

Newcastle's Literary and Philosophical Society moved into this splendid building in 1825, nearly thirty years after the Society (always affectionately known as the Lit and Phil) had been formed by the Reverend William Turner, and others. The foundation stone of the building was laid by the Duke of Sussex in 1822 followed by a grand celebration and dinner, thirty-five toasts and fifty-three speeches!

The Lit and Phil and its library became the centre of learning in Newcastle at that time, and the town's engineers, scientists and industrialists and others met there to discuss a variety of subjects. It was in this building that William Armstrong spoke on electricity in 1844, and Joseph Wilson Swan demonstrated the first incandescent lightbulb in 1880. Past presidents of the Society include the great engineers, Robert Stephenson, William Armstrong, and Charles Parsons.

Books were always at the heart of the Society's interests, even though some early practices seem strange today. The first catalogues were sorted by the size of books, and it was only in 1891 that the revolutionary decision was made to purchase novels, which now form a significant part of the library's collection of 150,000 books.

The building was nearly destroyed by fire in 1893, just a few hours after a lecture on electricity by Lord Armstrong, but was fully restored and is still flourishing today.

This drawing was drawn especially for the Lit and Phil. With its close proximity to the newspaper's offices and rich collection of information for the captions he would sometimes write for his drawings, the Lit and Phil was a magnet to Dawson throughout his period as an illustrator for the *North Mail*.

Victoria Square, Jesmond, 1938

When this drawing of Jesmond's Victoria Square appeared in 1938 its caption writer could not possibly have anticipated how much more significant his words would later become. Under the headline A LINK WITH VICTORIAN NEWCASTLE he wrote: 'Not far is one of the city's busiest traffic points.' The busy traffic point in his day was the junction between the north end of the square and Jesmond Road, then a major route into the city from the east. Nowadays the square has to live with an elevated section of the Central Motorway (East) whose construction in the 1970s caused the removal of all but this side. The Victoria Square of the drawing encircled an area of trees and lawns in which residents could relax. It was occupied by academics from nearby Armstrong College, professional people, and a sprinkling of city shop and store owners, who could easily walk to work from here. Dawson himself lived here briefly. Today, and for many years before its part demolition, it has been divided into flats, and while clearly visible to motorists travelling north on the motorway above, the remaining section is almost hidden from Sandyford Road.

Westgate Road, 1935

This view up Westgate Road from just opposite St John's Church to its junction with Fenkle Street, must have proved a challenging subject for even an accomplished architectural draughtsman. From Dawson's position on the pavement beside the fishing tackle shop of Bagnall & Kirkwood on the south side of Westgate Road, the central feature of the drawing is the white bulk of Cross House, only 24 years old but already the survivor of one of the city's worst fire disasters. On 23 December 1919 the famous Laskey film service, which housed tons of celluloid film in its basement, caught fire, claiming the lives of eleven people.

To the right of the restored building the County Court and the Trustees Savings Bank project from behind the tower of St John's. On the opposite side of the street its original fine town houses were by now converted into busy shops with offices above. The flags left, right and centre were still fluttering two weeks after the day of triumph and pageantry with which King George V and Queen Mary celebrated their Silver Jubilee in London. A loyal Newcastle acknowledged the occasion by bedecking every major building in the city with the national flag (see also the photograph on page 4).

Bigg Market, 1926

Probably one of the best-known parts of Newcastle, thanks to today's lively social scene, the Bigg Market of 1926 was fairly respectable, and noted for its street stalls and Sunday night orators rather than revellers. A market for a particular type of barley known as 'bigg' had been held here every Tuesday and Saturday from the early seventeenth century, and it gradually developed as a popular market for everything from crockery to livestock, extending right up into Newgate Street.

By 1926 the market stopped short at Grainger Street, and soon tramlines would restrict it to just one side. The Town Hall towers over the scene. The domed structure peeping over the stalls in the centre, is the J. H. Rutherford Memorial Fountain, erected in 1894 in St Nicholas Square, but moved here in 1903. It has now been moved to the Grainger Street end of the Bigg Market.

These men and women are demonstrating in the Bigg Market at the J.H. Rutherford Memorial Fountain *(just peeping over the stalls in the centre of the drawing opposite)*, before the start of the North East Contingent of Unemployed Marchers to London, 7 April, 1930.

City Hall and Baths, 1935

When Newcastle's City Hall was opened in 1928 as part of the first public building complex to be constructed after the First World War, nobody could have been more delighted than Dawson, a lover of classical music. Its construction on Northumberland Road, together with the integral public baths, did not quite meet the approval of local architects and planners as it neared completion. 'Not grand enough' was their view, one endorsed by Nikolaus Pevsner in his *Buildings of England: Northumberland*, 1957: 'a dull neo-Georgian design' he called it. But despite initial criticism both buildings became popular with the public, and were shortly after joined by Metrovick House further along the road towards Northumberland Street.

In the early days the City Hall was a venue for touring orchestras like the Berlin Philharmonic, but by the 1960s it had also become the place to see and hear some of the top groups in the charts. Its dominant position for concert performances has been challenged over the years, by the Mayfair Ballroom on Newgate Street, the Metro Radio (formerly Telewest) Arena off Scotswood Road, and then by the Sage Music Centre opened in 2004 at Gateshead Quays.

Hood Street, 1937

'Short yet dignified' read the caption to this drawing – a description still fitting today, despite the rebuilding of part of the north side of Hood Street. In 1937 the street was the location of two of the city's best-known buildings – the Tyne Temperance Hotel, on the far left, and the Church Institute. The hotel's guests could rejoice in distancing themselves from the evils of drink – ever present in the city at that time – while the Institute's visitors could enjoy a Musical Conversazioni, or one of Newcastle's annual fine art exhibitions sponsored by the Northumbria Art Institute, under the management of the Bewick Club.

Today the users of its buildings are rather different to those of the late 1930s, and Dawson would have hated the extension of Commercial Union House that today dominates the view of Pilgrim Street. The Temperance Hotel is now the home of the Northern Counties Club, which formerly stood in Eldon Square.

Broad Chare, Quayside, 1927

So called because, unlike the other narrow passageways called 'chares' which reached like tentacles from the Quayside into the dark masses of old buildings along the river bank, it could accommodate a horse-drawn wagon, Broad Chare retains some of its quaintness to this day. In 1927 the was still a canyon of soot-blackened warehouses, seedy public houses and curtainless tenements. It might easily have been mistaken for a Parisian backstreet rather than a vital link between the Tyne and the busy streets of the city beyond.

Broad Chare's jewel then, as now, was Trinity House, the ancient headquarters of the Master Pilots and Seamen and one of Newcastle's oldest institutions. Through an archway on the left of the Chare it is one of the most fascinating buildings in the city, with an unique collection of nautical artefacts ranging from a model of HMS *Victory* made of beef bones by British prisoners of war, to a mahogany table made for Nelson from a log he sat on himself.

The scene today has changed considerably as the Quayside has been transformed from the sad spectacle of grimy office buildings and decaying warehouses it had become in the 1960s into an area of smart apartments, restaurants and pubs. Broad Chare now boasts Live Theatre – converted from property owned by Trinity House in the early 1990s, and extended in 2007. On the eastern side of the entrance to the Chare is the Law Courts building, the first major building of the Quayside revival.

Blackfriars, Monk Street, 1936

When this drawing was published, this ancient building was actually the residence of several families. Its previous occupants – several of the town's craft companies – had decided to move out and let the premises. However, the squalor into which the building had descended by 1936 led to the re-housing of the families, and the building was gradually acquired by the City Council.

When Dawson stood on what is today named Friar's Green, to make this drawing, the role of the building as housing, not to mention its dilapidation, was clearly in evidence. However, many years were to elapse before plans for its restoration were drawn up. Restoration began in 1975, following extensive excavation of the surrounding site, and completed by 1981.

Today this area has been described as 'one of the most appealing public spaces in Newcastle'. The remaining buildings house craft shops and a restaurant, and the headquarters of the North East Civic Trust, with direct access from Monk Street on the west. Meanwhile much of the environment around the walls of Blackfriars has been sympathetically developed.

Quayside Sunday Market, 1936

In June 1936 Newcastle's colourful Sunday Market on the Quayside had just escaped threatened abolition under proposed new Sunday trading laws that would affect the freedom of corner shops to remain open on Sundays. However, as the newspaper caption declared: 'A promise was given in the House of Commons recently that the new Sunday Trading Act would be so phrased as not to jeopardise the holding of the market, which is the rendezvous of hundreds of Tynesiders.'

Drawn from Sandgate at the east end of the Quay, the scene had been transformed eight years earlier by the completion of the New Tyne Bridge. The throng of visitors was lured there by cheap goods. Street attractions, like strongmen, racing tipsters, and street artists, made it as much a fairground as a market. This was still part of the busy Port of Tyne – one of the vessels in this view is a pleasure boat from which spectators were taking in the scene before sailing for North Shields.

There is still a Sunday market at the Quayside, but it is much smaller, and a lot less interesting than the one pictured here, though the Quayside itself is always busy with visitors.

All Saints' Church, 1926

This view of All Saints, one of the few elliptical churches in Britain, had only recently been made possible by the clearance of the slums spilling from the area right of the drawing down to the Quayside. Here some of Newcastle's poorest inhabitants once lived in grossly overcrowded conditions, and the area was noted for its repeated epidemics of diseases such as typhus.

Built on the site of the twelfth-century Church of All Hallows, All Saints is the master work of little celebrated local architect David Stephenson (1757-1819), the first Newcastle architect to study in London. He won the competition to design the church at the age of just 29. Although the main part of the building was ready for consecration in 1789 he had to wait until 1796 to see its delicate steeple completed. However his wait was rewarded with a spectacle which was the talk of Tyneside for many years to come. Just before the weather vane was installed, a local soldier named John Burdikin climbed the scaffolding and did a handstand on the spire and remained in that position, 195 feet above the ground, for some time!

Town Moor Festival, 1937

One of his final illustrations for the *Sunday Sun*, in June 1937, this lively drawing of the Town Moor Hoppings at Race Week fronted a special supplement captioned THE TOWN MOOR FESTIVAL. Dawson's viewpoint from the top of one of the Festival's towering attractions captures all the excited bustle of the occasion as hundreds of Tyneside families flocked to this major annual event.

Founded in 1882 as the Town Moor Temperance Festival, an alternative to the drinking and gambling delights of Gosforth Park Races, the Hoppings had been held here continuously, except for a period between 1914 and 1923 when it was moved to Jesmond Vale. By the time this drawing appeared it had long established itself as the world's largest non-permanent fair, its brash music, noise and petrol fumes wafting over the city. 1937 had witnessed a succession of events to celebrate the coronation of George VI on 12 May, and the festive atmosphere might have given more of a sense of occasion to that year's Hoppings.

The Town Moor Hoppings was a favourite subject of local artists, none more so than Dawson. Several of his studies in oil and watercolour are in the collection of the Laing Art Gallery.

Maling Ford (B) Pottery, Walker, 1935

When Dawson sketched this scene in January 1935 Maling's busy workers would scarcely have noticed him. At the height of productivity, making thousands of pieces for its major client, Ringtons Tea, it was also turning out commemorative ware for the Silver Jubilee of George V and Queen Mary, and time was precious. Published as part of his series on prominent local industries, Maling's was one of Tyneside's best-known employers and had an impressively large workforce. Thanks to Ringtons, the largest door-to-door tea distribution company in the UK, its distinctive products had made it a household name in thousands of North East homes. Maling had a long tradition with commemorative ware. Patterns for other pieces produced by its predominantly female labour force that year ran into dozens, with a kaleidoscope of colours, but special care was taken with the Jubilee items. The company produced a special wall plaque picturing the royals which, like many Maling pieces, is now a rare collectors' item.

Maling's Ford (B) Pottery is no more. Production in the closing years of the 1930s gradually dropped and in 1947 the company was sold to Hoults Estates Ltd who closed the pottery in 1963.

Stephenson's Monument, Westgate Road, 1937

Just a stone's throw from the newspaper offices on the left, this view of the junction of Westgate Road, Neville Street and Collingwood Street would be one all too familiar to Dawson. The scene of one of Newcastle's largest ever public gatherings in 1862, when 100,000 people assembled to witness the unveiling of the monument to George Stephenson, was now ONE OF NEWCASTLE'S BUSIEST JUNCTONS.

Dawson drew this view with his back to the famous Long Bar running from Westgate Road to Neville Street. On the right is Neville Hall, the home of the Mining Institute, dating back to 1872, and just beyond it the slightly projecting façade of the Lit & Phil building of 1825. The Sun Insurance Building, just beyond the statue, on the corner of Collingwood Street, dates to 1904, and on the opposite corner Collingwood Buildings was completed in 1899.

Much has changed to the left of the drawing since it was published. After the departure of the newspaper offices to the Groat Market in 1965, a massive office block, now removed, was built on the site. In the foreground, the Grainger Memorial Fountain set up next to Stephenson's statue in 1892, was removed in the 1950s. Its water trough for carriage horses was replaced by a taxi rank!

Newcastle Breweries, Bath Lane, 1935

In January 1935, when the first in the series *An Artist tours the Industrial North* appeared, Newcastle Breweries was just recovering from a national decline in beer sales of 34 per cent, following the General Strike of 1926. The North East region was one of the worst hit areas in the Depression, but either as a morale boost to *North Mail* readers, or a genuine recognition that things were now getting better, the series not only took Dawson to the Bath Lane premises of the brewery but to those of all the leading local manufacturing companies, including shipyards, factories and even its best-known pottery – Maling.

This view shows just a small part of the brewery's twenty-acre Gallowgate site. Founded in 1884, its buildings were so numerous and spacious that Dawson would be allowed to use its lofts to complete large oil paintings. By 1960 the world-famous Scottish & Newcastle Breweries, with its thriving chain of pubs and hotels, needed a new HQ. The high-rise block, opposite the football ground, completed in 1965, remained the HQ until 2004, when production of its iconic and last remaining locally brewed beer, Newcastle Brown Ale, was transferred to the Federation Brewery in Gateshead. The brewing of Newcastle Brown Ale has now been relocated to Yorkshire, ending an association with the area dating back to 1927.

St Nicholas' Vestry (Thomlinson Library), 1936

This 1736 addition to the south side of St Nicholas' Church was regarded for many years as an 'incongruous edifice', but by 1936 the vestry to the (by then) cathedral was a cherished part of one of the city's oldest buildings. Sir Walter Blackett provided funds to build the vestry, which incorporated a two-storey library to house the books of the Rev Dr Thomlinson and other benefactors. Over the years the collection deteriorated, and in 1888 it was moved to the city's new Free Library on New Bridge Street. In 1926 a hall, library and new vestry were added to the building, with staircase access from the chancel. The view was taken just yards from the site of Thomas Bewick's second workshop.

In the caption Dawson remarked that the view would be enhanced by the removal of the railings surrounding the ancient graveyard. They had recently been put up to protect the area from drunks and wayfarers and replaced the original (long-gone) railings that had protected the tombstones of the rich and famous. Today the scene has changed little since the drawing was made. The railings have long gone, apart from a strip added to the south side of the cathedral grounds around 1926, but not included in the drawing.

Marlborough Crescent, 1936

Marlborough Crescent was the location of two of Newcastle's most dramatic events of the early 1930s; the catastrophic burning of the King's Hall Cinema in 1931, and the city's first armed bank robbery at the nearby Market Keeper's House, in 1933.

By 1936 the old cattle market was being cleared to make way for the Marlborough Crescent Bus Station which would make the area one of the busiest in the city, with brightly coloured Venture Bus Company vehicles constantly streaming in and out. In time the increasing flow of city shop and office workers would make the area very prosperous, Clayton Street West, below the steeple of St Mary's Cathedral, was a particular beneficiary. Times change, however, and by the 1990s the bus station had gone, and the area had become an unofficial carpark.

Few sites in the city can claim to have been as dramatically redeveloped over the years as this one. Towering over today's Times Square stands the International Centre for Life. Completed in 2000, the development comprises three main buildings costing £60m, a major public attraction in addition to internationally renowned Human Genetics and Bioscience research facilities.

South African War Memorial, Haymarket, 1935

Dominating the Haymarket since its unveiling in June 1908, by the mid-1930s the South African War Memorial had long been regarded as an outstanding piece of public sculpture. Dawson's friend and cinema owner, Dixon Scott, gave the artist permission to capture the view from a window of the Haymarket Cinema, which opened in 1933. The drawing shows a relatively quiet scene. The monument, by sculptor Thomas Eyre Macklin, was the result of an open competition in which forty-one models were submitted. Sixty-eight feet tall it was financed by the Northumberland War Fund and cost around £2,000.

By the mid-1930s Northumberland Street had become one of the most traffic-laden in the city, linking the New Tyne Bridge to the A1 Great North Road. Trolley buses would join and later challenge the dominance of the tramcar from 1935. The scaffolded building on the left became a bank, while the Haymarket Bus Station, opened by 1939, provided opportunities for a wide range of surrounding businesses, including shops, cafes, and even another cinema – The Tatler. The 1970s Metro station now dominates the area.

The Fruit and Vegetable Market, St Andrew's Street, 1935

Part of Dawson's brief series for the *Sunday Sun*, '*How the North Lives and Plays*', this scene must have been familiar to its readers as hundreds of city dwellers flocked daily to buy the fresh produce. The drawing probably shows a Saturday evening when stall holders were marking down their prices dramatically. The Market then was a cavernous place where wholesalers haggled with retail customers. The location was one of the city's busiest and most congested, the wholesalers with their premises on both sides of St Andrew's Street ran teams of barrowmen shuttling between unloading vehicles and their warehouses. Later in the day, the barrowmen would distribute orders to waiting stall holders in the market building.

Sometimes referred to simply as the Green Market, it had begun its days as an outdoor affair on Newgate Street outside St Andrew's Church. By the 1960s the open sides and cobbled floor of the purpose-built Market Hall were increasingly inconvenient and the level of traffic unacceptable. In 1968 the wholesaling business was transferred to a new covered market in the Team Valley, while the retail side moved to the Grainger Market, and later to part of the Eldon Square shopping development.

High Friar Street, 1925

Yet another street swallowed up by the Eldon Square shopping development, High Friar Street featured in Dawson's *Characteristic Corners of Newcastle* series, possibly because it was representative of the many narrow back streets which intersected the city. The caption to the drawing, taken from the corner of Clayton Street looking east reads: ' … another admirable example of a characteristic and picturesque corner of Newcastle … The composition is strikingly successful and the draughtsmanship characterised by admirable restraint.'

High Friar Street then boasted several public houses, two of which, the Bacchus on its corner with Newgate Street, and the Crown & Sceptre, known as Curley's Bar, were among the most popular in the area. But the street had earlier achieved celebrity as the birthplace of the North East's greatest-ever woodcarver, Gerrard Robinson, who was born there in 1834, the son of Robert Robinson, a blacksmith. Robinson's birthplace, thought to have been in the section between Newgate and Clayton Streets, had long disappeared by 1925, the victim of an earlier development.

This section of the street lay roughly along the line of Eldon Square's Sidgate Mall. The building whose rounded end features right, still stands on the corner of Nelson Street and Clayton Street, now just part of the façade of the shopping development running along Nelson Street's northern side.

Glasshouse Bridge, 1926

The last major bridge over the Ouseburn before it enters the Tyne, Glasshouse Bridge (opened in 1878) looked down on a scene that its caption remarked was 'almost Continental', with its mix of river vessels and old warehouses. The Ouseburn here was a working part of the Tyne, its mouth a mooring point for barges called 'wherries', which used the tidal action of the river to navigate as far up as Byker Bridge. Those pictured in the foreground were among the last used in this way to carry bulk materials to the industries upstream. They disappeared in the 1950s as these industries declined, and houseboats replaced them at this convenient mooring point on the lower Tyne.

The warehouses have all gone, including that of the Tyne Tees Shipping Company on the right. Were it not for the still towering presence of Glasshouse Bridge, and the lower bridge built in 1908, the scene might well be unrecognisable. The pagoda-like domes of what were, until the late 1970s, the Council Schools, still punctuate the skyline, but the area around the mouth of the burn has been tastefully landscaped and now features the Ouseburn Barrage, opened in 2009. A lock that forms part of the development enables houseboats and other users to pass under the arches into what looks like a canal – the days of waiting for the tide to allow this movement are gone and there is permanent berthing in deep water instead of boats ending up high and dry at low tide.

Eldon Square, 1935

When Eldon Square was completed in 1831 by local developer Richard Grainger, its twenty-six elegant houses were regarded as the most prestigious and desirable residential properties in Newcastle. In *Buildings of England: Northumberland*, 1957, Nikolaus Pevsner described it: '... here indeed a claim to formality and monumentality was staked that was new to the town and must at once have doomed the modest houses of Saville Row ... The spaciousness of Eldon Square was something quite unheard of ...'

By the early 1900s the Square had begun to be colonised by businesses, until by 1935 only caretakers lived there full time. Just one original tenant remained, Newcastle's oldest gentlemen's club, The Northern Counties, at No. 13 on the extreme right of the drawing. The appearance of the buildings had also changed, provoking Pevsner to write: 'The execrable top excrescences of many of the houses ought to disappear without delay.'

Many understandably opposed the demolition of the western and central sections of the Square in 1973 to make way for the Eldon Square shopping development, but vast expenditure, and strict control of the tenants, would have been needed to stop the buildings deteriorating further.

Today, an attractive green public space surrounds the 1923 First World War memorial.

Blackett Street, 1936

With the headline WHERE NEWCASTLE TURNS, this drawing of the junction of Blackett Street and
Northumberland Street captures a scene which, since the opening of the New Tyne Bridge eight years earlier,
had become the most traffic congested in the city. Now effectively part of the Great North Road,
Northumberland Street and Pilgrim Street had become a highway for north-south vehicles, while Blackett
Street had to cope with those arriving not only from west and east, but feeding in from Grey and Grainger
Streets. The shop on the right was the giant Lowe and Moorhouse store, while dominating the centre is the
onion-domed YMCA, built in 1889. The traffic must have been a nightmare for the policeman controller,
pictured right in his distinctive black uniform and hat. He not only had to cope with the rise in private car
ownership of the 1930s, but the cross-town movement of trams, and the increasing throngs of shoppers and
city workers heading in all directions. The popular YMCA building, with its restaurant, and gym, was
demolished in 1972 for the new Eldon Square shopping development.

Eldon Place, Barras Bridge, 1938

It was only when he drew Eldon Place (at the Barras Bridge end of Eldon Street) for the *North Mail* that Dawson noticed a plaque identifying the home of famous locomotive engineer George Stephenson. The newspaper sub-editors apparently also thought it a revelation! The bold headline read: GEORGE STEPHENSON LIVED IN THIS 19TH CENTURY STREET IN BUSY NEWCASTLE, while the caption, as if disowning the discovery should it be incorrect reads: 'says *North Mail* artist Byron Dawson'.

George Stephenson moved to No. 17 Eldon Place in 1824, with his son Robert and second wife Elizabeth Hindmarsh, from Dial Cottage, Killingworth. In 1938 the Stephenson Residential Hotel was next door. The rest of the street was occupied by academics, professionals, and business premises – including a car showroom. The Stephensons' house has long vanished beneath University expansion. The railed area disappeared in the building of what was first the University Theatre and Gulbenkian Studio of 1969-70 (now Northern Stage) and all that remains of the street itself – overshadowed by the University's King's Gate – are two of its modest brick houses, and the former car showroom.

The Laing Art Gallery and Public Library, 1936

Busy New Bridge Street was the ideal location for the city's first 'Free Library', officially opened in 1884, and for the Laing Art Gallery, opened in 1904. By 1936 they formed what today might be described as 'the cultural hub' of the city.

When it opened, the Library already owned an impressive collection of over 20,000 books. They included the collection of the former Mechanics' Institute next door, and the Thomlinson Collection previously housed at St Nicholas's Cathedral. The Laing opened its entrance on Higham Place without a single picture or object of art, but by 1936 had amassed a substantial permanent collection mainly consisting of watercolours. In 1905 the gallery had initiated a series of Artists of the Northern Counties annual exhibitions providing local artists like Dawson a showcase.

The Library, whose projecting entrance is on the right of the drawing, was replaced in 1968 with a new building by architect Basil Spence on the west side of the newly created John Dobson Street. The Laing's entrance was later moved to New Bridge Street, and the area in front paved with Thomas Heatherwick's Blue Carpet. A splendid new City Library opened in 2009, on the footprint of the 1968 building.

Index of streets and buildings